Agnès Jaoui

Jean-Pierre Bacri

A FAMILY AFFAIR

Un Air de Famille

Adapted by

Andy de la Tour

OBERON BOOKS

LONDON

Adaptor's Note

Stumbling accidentally across the delightful French film *Un Air de Famille* I knew immediately I wanted to adapt and direct it for the theatre. Surprised to find the English-language rights still available – after all, the play upon which the film was based had enjoyed a successful run in Paris – I set about writing my version. The most immediate decision that needed to be made was whether to keep the play's location in France or move it to Britain. If this is a play about a typical family – what kind of family should it be? A typical English family perhaps, whatever that is? How about a family from an ethnic minority, north London Turkish Cypriot perhaps? But the obvious choice soon presented itself – why transpose the story at all? I loved *Un Air de Famille* because the Menard family – and the setting we find them in, a very ordinary bar – were so typically French. So I kept them French. Not *Allo, Allo* French but real French like they are in the original. So real in fact that you can't help thinking that you've been in this bar before. Somewhere on the road from Calais to Paris perhaps, at the beginning of that holiday you took years ago, when everyone in the car was clamouring for their first meal of *steak-frites* and cheap *vin de table*.

Working from an excellent literal translation by Sasha Mitchell (how many 'translated by…' credits in the theatre are actually writers working from literal translations I wonder…), I immediately realised how differently the characters would have to talk to make them sound authentic. For starters, the French use so many words, many more than we do. To find a rhythm of speech for the characters that would ring true – and funny into the bargain – nearly every speech had to be trimmed. English is a very economical language. Few words go far.

But no matter how good the literal translation, translated dialogue obliterates character. So I tried to create an individual voice for each member of the family without breaking faith with the authors' intentions. Not always easy. I was tempted to tone down the daughter Betty's language, because I felt she swore far too much and a British audience might take a strong dislike to her. Actually I was being far too 'English' – prudish in other words. In France, Betty's swearing would be typical of a young woman like her.

Having the original authors available at the end of a phone-line has its plusses and minuses. Adapting a dead writer's work may leave you lots of scope but in my experience it was good discipline to have to discuss – on occasion negotiate even – with Agnès Jaoui, the co-author with Jean-Pierre Bacri, my suggested departures from the original text. 'Adaptation' is an ambiguous word. In one respect *A Family Affair* is a true and faithful version of *Un Air de Famille*. Almost every single line of my dialogue can be identified from the original text; hardly one piece of conversation is wholly invented. But at the same time almost every line of my 'adaptation' is actually quite different from the original, on occasion quite far removed. But all in a good cause I hope. All I ever wanted is to do justice to the extraordinary colourful characters that are the Menard family in *Un Air de Famille*.

As if to prove an earlier point, a final word about the title. 'Un Air de Famille' is almost untranslatable. Meaning 'the appearance of a family' or 'family resemblance' none of the translated versions of the title exactly trip off the tongue. 'A family affair' is my best compromise offer. Not a translation at all of course but an 'adaptation' of the title that hopefully captures the essence of this wonderful play.

Andy de la Tour
London, 2000

Characters

BETTY

DENIS

HENRI

MADAME MENARD

PHILIPPE

YOLANDE

A Family Affair was first performed at the Regent Theatre, Stoke-on-Trent on 17 October 2000, with the following cast:

BETTY, Rachel Power

DENIS, Neil McKinven

HENRI, Rik Mayall

MADAME MENARD, Anne Reid

PHILIPPE, Steven Pacey

YOLANDE, Susan Wooldridge

Director, Andy de la Tour

Designer, Saul Radomsky

ACT ONE

An ordinary bar in a provincial town in France. Early evening in summer. At one end of the serving bar itself, a swing-door to the kitchen and the private quarters upstairs. A phone at the other end. An arch leads off to a slightly smarter area for eating. There's an old-fashioned jukebox, a few barstools and some tables and chairs. A door leads down to the cellar and the toilets. By the jukebox a dog basket is just visible, with two large dog paws hanging over the edge.

A woman, BETTY, 30, sits on her own near the entrance, smoking a cigarette. Music from the jukebox. An out of date dance track, sung in (bad) English by a French band.

DENIS, mid 30s, sweeps up near the empty tables. He moves slightly to the music, singing quietly along with it. Suddenly the music stops. DENIS goes over to the jukebox and gives it a hefty punch. Twice. The music starts up again. He continues sweeping, this time nearer to BETTY's table. He sings slightly louder this time. She looks up, without smiling. He smiles at her. No response from BETTY. Suddenly the music stops again. DENIS leaves the music off. BETTY finishes her drink. DENIS puts the broom to one side, takes out his tea-towel and goes back over to BETTY.

DENIS: Would the young lady like anything else?

> *BETTY just shakes her head.*

Sure she wouldn't like another drink?

BETTY: No. This is fine. Thanks.

> *DENIS clears a couple of glasses away from the empty table next to her. He then goes back to her.*

DENIS: She'd really like another little Suze, wouldn't she?

BETTY: No. She wouldn't. Thank you.

DENIS: The young lady seems a little pissed off.

BETTY: Denis – for God's sake.

He sits next to her.

DENIS: You're angry, aren't you?

BETTY: No. I'm not angry.

DENIS: Yes, you are. I can tell.

BETTY: No. I'm not.

DENIS: So you must be happy then?

BETTY: Yeah, well, actually I am. I've got a good reason to be.

DENIS: Yeah?

BETTY: I told my boss what I thought of him. I've been dying to do it for months. So, yeah, as it happens I'm happy.

DENIS: Benito? You're kidding?

BETTY: Yeah.

DENIS: (*Whistles.*) Your brother wasn't there, was he?

BETTY: No, he missed it. He'll die when I tell him.

DENIS: You mean he'll die laughing?

BETTY: Yeah.

DENIS: You really think so?

BETTY: 'Course he will. He's been longing for someone to stand up to that dickhead. Benito's always made Philippe feel about that small.

BETTY gestures tiny.

DENIS: You're fond of your little Philippe, aren't you?

BETTY: What's that supposed to mean?

DENIS: Well… Philippe this, Philippe that…

BETTY: He's my brother.

DENIS: So's Henri your brother.

BETTY: So what? …I've got more in common with
Philippe… We work together for a start…

DENIS: I'm just saying. (*Pause.*) I'm, uh, I'm free later on.

BETTY: So?

DENIS: Well, we can…y'know? …if you want, we can…

BETTY: What about Wednesday?

DENIS: Wednesday?

BETTY: Wednesday, Denis. You were supposed to phone me.

DENIS: Were we supposed to phone each other?

BETTY: No we weren't supposed to phone each other.
You were supposed to phone me.

DENIS: Yeah? Really?

BETTY: Yeah, really.

DENIS: Did I say I would? (*She looks.*) Did I say like
'I'd phone'? I mean in those words.

BETTY looks at him.

I s'pose I must have done. I don't remember.

BETTY: I don't remember either. Jesus, what a depressing
conversation.

DENIS: You could have phoned me.

She looks at him.

BETTY: Denis.

DENIS: Yeah?

9

BETTY: Let's finish this.

DENIS: What? Finish what?

BETTY: This. You and me. This crappy relationship. Let's call it a day, yeah? I mean nothing'll actually change but at least we'll know where we stand.

DENIS: 'This crappy relationship'. Is that what – what – we – you think we –

BETTY: It's just an expression.

DENIS: Pretty powerful expression.

BETTY: Well…'flimsy relationship' if you prefer.

DENIS: I think I do prefer 'flimsy relationship', yeah. I mean up to a point. Well…okay, if that's what you want, it's – it's up to you.

BETTY: As usual.

DENIS: But I thought, y'know, we were okay… You know, we'd see each other but at the same time we were… y'know? Did you expect it to be…y'know? …different?

BETTY: I didn't expect it to be anything, Denis. You and me are very similar, I'm not asking you to marry me. I mean I've got my life too – but if you say you're going to phone me then phone me!

DENIS sits there anxiously, not sure what to say. He is quite inadvertently rubbing his knee with his tea-towel. HENRI appears from the door that leads to the kitchen and upstairs. He's 40 and one of BETTY's older brothers. He comes straight over to her.

HENRI: How long you been here?

BETTY: Ten – fifteen minutes.

They greet each other – two kisses on each cheek.

HENRI: You know, you and Mum sound exactly the same. I was getting ready just now and I thought 'Shit, they're here already'.

BETTY: Hey, you've got on your little Friday jumper.

HENRI wears a sleeveless jumper over his shirt and tie. He feels a little self-conscious about it.

HENRI: What else d'you expect me to wear?

He looks at DENIS who's still rubbing his knee with his tea-towel.

That knee clean enough yet?

DENIS realises and then stops.

Spotless. Now go and finish up.

DENIS gets up and wanders off into the kitchen. HENRI goes over to the dog in the basket. He leans over him.

Yes, yes, yes, yes, yes…you're hungry, aren't you? Yes you are. Din dins is on its way. Daddy'll bring you din dins, yes he will, yes he will.

BETTY: Where's Arlette? Getting ready?

HENRI: Uh, no, she's… God knows where she is. It's a quarter to eight and she's not even back yet. No, I know where she's got to. Gossiping with her mate, that's where. Yak yak yak.

HENRI has gone over to the bar and busies himself. BETTY goes to the bar and sits on a stool.

BETTY: Love is a many splendid thing.

HENRI: What the fuck's that supposed to mean?

BETTY: The way you talk about Arlette. So tender. So understanding.

HENRI: Betty, what do you know about it? You ever lived
with someone? No, 'course you haven't. Go and live with
someone for fifteen years and then come and talk to me
about understanding. Know what your trouble is? You
watch too many films. You think life's a movie. And him.
He thinks you get it from books.

DENIS: Leave me out of this.

*DENIS has returned and is cleaning up at the other end of
the bar.*

HENRI: They're on their way right now so where the hell
is she? She knows Friday night's family night... How'd
she think it makes me look like when they get here and
she's not even here? On a Friday. Like some sad git who
can't even control his bloody wife, that's what. Yeah,
well, I tell you something, Betty. I'm not Dad. No one's
going to walk all over me. I mean don't get me wrong,
I love Arlette. I love my wife. But I tell you something
for nothing... I'm too nice a bloke as it is.

He notices DENIS smirking.

What's the hell's so funny? You saying I'm wrong?

DENIS: I – I don't know, I'm...neutral.

HENRI: No, no, out with it! Say what you think. Come on.

DENIS: I'd prefer not to...commit myself.

BETTY: He'd prefer not to commit himself. He's neutral.
I can answer for him if you like, Henri.

HENRI: No, no, no, that's fine, I know what you think
already. With all that woman stuff. Wind you up and off
you go. Talk non-stop for an hour and it's all bollocks
anyway.

BETTY: Well, I'm a woman. I know what we're like.

HENRI: Yeah, well so do I. Women are women and men are
men.

DENIS: Can't argue with that.

HENRI: It's human nature, why mess around with it? Your giraffe, you want your giraffe, yes you do, yes you do.

HENRI brings out a small squeaking giraffe which he squeaks as he takes it over to the dog.

Hey. I was watching the tennis on the TV, right? Know what I saw? A woman in shorts. A professional tennis player in shorts. You call that normal?

DENIS: A woman in shorts. Do I call that normal?

HENRI: Yeah, a professional tennis player!

DENIS: Uh… I've never really thought about it. Depends on the shorts, I suppose. I mean I've seen different women in different shorts of course –

HENRI: Don't be such a prick. A professional woman tennis player!

DENIS: You'd have preferred her in a little skirt, right?

HENRI: Too right I'd have preferred her in a little skirt! Jesus.

BETTY and DENIS exchange a smile.

BETTY: I think I will have another drink. What the hell, it's Friday.

DENIS pours her another drink.

HENRI: Same goes for you too. Acting a little ladylike every now and again wouldn't hurt.

BETTY: Next time I'll wear a little skirt.

HENRI: You sound like a man, the way you talk. And drink, look at you. You're never going to get anyone that way, Betty, believe me. Listen, let me tell you something for your own good. You don't catch flies with vinegar. Mmm? And time's not on your side, know what I mean?

BETTY: Henri, that's – what do I say? Thanks. Terrific.

HENRI: 'S nothing.

BETTY: No, that's a great help. I really needed something to put me on the right track – and you've come up with it. 'You don't catch flies with vinegar'. You've no idea how much that helps. Amazing, isn't it? How a proverb can change your life.

HENRI's not sure if she's taking the piss.

You always say you don't want people to think you're stupid, right? Well that requires some effort on your part too, Henri, okay?

BETTY wanders off with her drink. HENRI turns to DENIS and smiles nervously.

HENRI: Did you get any of that?

DENIS: Uh uh. Everything.

HENRI: Is she upset, d'you think?

DENIS: Uh uh.

HENRI: Yeah, well…'truth hurts'.

DENIS: No, no, that's…that's nonsense, boss. That's the sort of thing you say when you're fourteen.

HENRI: Yeah, okay, well, if a brother can't be honest with his sister…

DENIS carries on polishing the beer pump.

How long you going to keep polishing that for?

DENIS: It's got to shine, hasn't it? Otherwise why bother? If there's one thing that's really got to shine in a bar, it's the beer pump.

HENRI busies himself but turns back.

HENRI: You think I'm an idiot too, don't you?

DENIS doesn't reply.

Just get the mop and clean the floor, Denis, alright?
Standing around arguing all the time. It's Friday.
We close early on Fridays remember?

DENIS: (*Going.*) You're the one asking all the questions.

HENRI: (*Suddenly.*) Shit! Fuckit!!

*BETTY looks up. HENRI looks at the clock. DENIS returns
immediately from the kitchen with the mop and bucket.*

I completely forgot. Bollocks.

DENIS: What's the matter?

HENRI: Just – just – just get on with the floor, will you?
You're not Napoleon, you know? You can't talk *and* mop
the floor at the same time.

DENIS: Did Napoleon mop floors?

HENRI looks at him. DENIS takes the mop to the floor.

HENRI: I forgot to watch my brother.

DENIS: Watch your brother?

HENRI: At seven o'clock! He told me to watch him and
I forgot.

DENIS: What? He turned up here at seven and said
'watch me'?

HENRI: Don't be such a prick! On the TV! He was on the
– what d'you call it? The local news thing. At seven. But
I turned the TV *off* at seven! When that quiz programme
I watch finished! I completely forgot about it.

DENIS: How come he was on television?

HENRI: How come he was on television?

DENIS: Yeah.

HENRI: You're joking. Don't you know who my brother is? 'How come?' Tssch. Betty, did you – did you see him?

BETTY is standing over by the window with her drink, looking out. HENRI comes over to her.

Come on, talk to me. Look, I'm sorry, you are, you're very…feminine, really – now did you see him?

BETTY: Of course.

HENRI: 'Of course'. Well it was easy for you to remember, wasn't it? You work with him all day. So…you saw it, yeah?

BETTY: Uh uh.

HENRI: Well… I'll tell him I saw it too. What was it, uh, what was it like then?

BETTY: Are you going to lie?

HENRI: Of course I'm going to lie! D'you think I can tell him I forgot when Mum phoned me only an hour before to remind me it was on! It just went completely out of my head, *I* don't know why. The quiz finished and… So…what was it like then? What – what did he say? What was he wearing?

DENIS: And what was the presenter wearing, what was the set like –

HENRI: That's good, yeah, all that sort of stuff.

BETTY: D'you think he's going to test you on it?

HENRI: Yeah, well, you never know. Philippe said 'I'm on television tomorrow' and Mum called only an hour before. Means they want to know what I think, right?

BETTY: Not necessarily. It means he just wanted you to watch it, that's all. He told everybody. He phoned round the whole family, I mean that's natural. What d'you want him to ask you? I mean what do you know about the computer business?

HENRI: Oh right, I get it, 'cos I'm too stupid, right?

BETTY: Oh Henri –

HENRI: The family idiot, that's me! You don't think Philippe's going to ask *me* anything?? 'Course he isn't!

BETTY: Did I say that??

HENRI: I've heard it a thousand times! The same old tune. You, Mum, Philippe. No, don't bother to ask Henri, what does he know? He's too thick to understand fuck all!

BETTY: Stop it! That isn't true!

HENRI: You think so? Denis, is it true or not?

DENIS: Me again. Why always me?

HENRI: Who else am I going to ask?

DENIS: Fine. What was the question?

HENRI: Am I the family idiot?

DENIS: Yes.

HENRI: See! Told you.

HENRI goes behind the bar. DENIS shrugs at BETTY. HENRI counts the money up in the till. BETTY lights another cigarette and sips her drink.

Is this all you've taken since three o'clock this afternoon?

DENIS: It was quiet.

HENRI: You can say that again.

DENIS: I spent most of the afternoon reading. I was hardly disturbed at all.

HENRI: Don't look too upset about it, will you?

DENIS carries on. BETTY comes closer to HENRI.

BETTY: Things are pretty slow at the moment then?

HENRI: Slow? This place. We got two speeds. Slow and Stop. Few lunchtime regulars…

He wanders over to the dog.

Yes, yes, yes, yes, yes, you're going to have your din dins very soon but then you got to stay here and have a good nighty-night's sleep 'cos Daddy's going out, yes he is, because Daddy goes out Fridays but he'll be right back for his little Caruso. (*To BETTY.*) He'd like to come with us but…

BETTY: Christ, I'm sick of the Duc de Bretagne. Couldn't we go somewhere else for a change?

HENRI: How can you be sick of it? It's the best restaurant around. It's got a – a – what the fuck d'you call them?

DENIS: A star.

HENRI: A star, that's it.

MADAME MENARD comes into the café, closely followed by PHILIPPE and YOLANDE. MADAME MENARD is BETTY's mother. PHILIPPE is BETTY's other brother, a couple of years younger than HENRI. YOLANDE is his wife and today's her birthday. MADAME MENARD goes straight towards the stairs leading to the basement.

MADAME MENARD: I'm absolutely dying for a pee. Nobody lurking down here, is there?

Before HENRI can reply she's down the stairs. PHILIPPE and HENRI kiss to exchange greetings, as do YOLANDE and BETTY.

PHILIPPE: What's it mean when it goes 'tick tick tick' like that? Near the wheels. When I steer to the right, 'tick tick tick tick', what d'you think?

HENRI: It's the indicator.

PHILIPPE: Don't be stupid. Near the wheels, 'tick tick tick tick'.

HENRI: Why you asking me? How should I know? Ask a mechanic.

PHILIPPE greets BETTY as HENRI greets YOLANDE.

PHILIPPE: It's so annoying, it's a brand new car as well.

BETTY: Hey, well done. I saw you, it was great.

PHILIPPE: Did you? Did you think it was good?

YOLANDE: I told him it was good.

PHILIPPE: (*Ignoring YOLANDE.*) Honestly? Because I can't judge, I don't know what to think any more.

BETTY: Yeah, absolutely. Well I suppose the only thing you might say was he didn't let you talk very much.

YOLANDE: I told him that too but –

PHILIPPE: (*Cutting her off.*) He kept cutting me off. I was only saying that to Mum in the car. I even told him at one point, didn't I? I said, 'Let me finish'.

BETTY: (*Being helpful.*) You did, I remember.

PHILIPPE: But they rush you. They ask you a question, then they ask you the next one before you've answered the first one.

HENRI: Terrible.

PHILIPPE: It's very unsettling. But I dunno, I think I got the main points across.

The others agree, especially HENRI.

HENRI: You did, definitely.

PHILIPPE: I mentioned the company name four or five times –

YOLANDE: (*Proud.*) Five.

HENRI: At least.

PHILIPPE: – but other than that, I mean, who knows?

BETTY: Yeah, right.

HENRI: Television. Huh.

PHILIPPE: Right.

A slight hiatus. BETTY suddenly starts to tickle YOLANDE.

BETTY: Hey! Happy Birthday!

PHILIPPE: No, no, it's not yet!

BETTY: What? (*Confused.*) When is it?

PHILIPPE: Later, when we're at the restaurant. When we're all together.

PHILIPPE takes a couple of chairs off a table. Chairs that DENIS has just put up on the table.

Let's sit down for five minutes.

PHILIPPE offers BETTY a chair but ignores YOLANDE who has to get her own chair from off the table.

Where's Arlette? Isn't she here?

HENRI: Yeah… No, she's…she's in the middle of…

PHILIPPE: So you saw it, yes?

HENRI: Uh, yep. Yeah.

PHILIPPE: So…was I…you know? …Did I make sense?

HENRI: Uh…did you make sense?

PHILIPPE: Yeah, did I make sense?

HENRI: Uh…

BETTY comes to the rescue.

BETTY: It's only a silly thing…but at one point you stuttered slightly.

YOLANDE: See?

HENRI: (*Latching on.*) Yeah, right. You stuttered.

PHILIPPE: I stuttered?

HENRI: At one point.

PHILIPPE: That's the bit you remember, is it?

HENRI looks at BETTY and then back at PHILIPPE. But MADAME MENARD appears from downstairs.

MADAME MENARD: Henri, you cannot see the nose in front of your face on those stairs. Just waiting for someone to break their neck before we change the lightbulb, are we? (*Indicates DENIS.*) Why can't he go out and buy one?

She suddenly notices the dog and goes over.

Forgive me, my little Caruso, I haven't said hello to my little baby boy (*Baby talk.*) How are you today? Are you happy?

HENRI is beside her, joining in.

HENRI: Who's this then? Who's this then?

MADAME MENARD: She's your granny.

HENRI: Yes she is, yes she is.

PHILIPPE: (*To BETTY.*) So the only thing you noticed is me stuttering?

BETTY: Just once or twice, that's all, it wasn't...y'know?

PHILIPPE: Oh, it was twice now. He only said once.

MADAME MENARD rejoins the group. She and BETTY greet each other. PHILIPPE gets to his feet to get another chair off the tables for her.

MADAME MENARD: It was nothing, Philippe, a mere...blip. You came across very well, I told you –

YOLANDE: I told him too.

MADAME MENARD: – for someone who's not a professional. I was very proud of you. Even the baker saw you. He told me so himself.

PHILIPPE: Really? What – what did he say?

MADAME MENARD: Nothing. He just said he saw you. Henri, is there a reason it's like a sauna in here?

She sits down, fanning herself.

YOLANDE: Sauna? That's funny 'cos I'm quite cold.

PHILIPPE: How can you be cold? It's boiling in here, how can you say you're cold?

YOLANDE: Just a little bit, y'know?

MADAME MENARD: There was one thing of course –

PHILIPPE: Mum, please. Don't bring up the tie again, okay?

HENRI: The tie?

MADAME MENARD: No, no, if you don't want to talk about it that's fine. I just don't happen to think it's a tie you wear on television, that's all. It was far, far too... well, least said.

The others look at her.

YOLANDE: I told him this morning. I said 'Sweetheart, the bow-tie isn't right. It's too loud'. But he wouldn't listen. He didn't want my advice.

HENRI: (*To YOLANDE.*) I thought so as well. 'Loud'.

PHILIPPE has stood up. He's wearing his shirt open-necked. He takes the bow-tie out of his jacket pocket.

PHILIPPE: I stuttered, I was badly dressed –

MADAME MENARD: No one said you were badly dressed –

PHILIPPE: (*To HENRI.*) Anything else while you're at it?

HENRI thinks for a moment and shakes his head. PHILIPPE turns to DENIS who's quietly mopping the floor still.

What about you? What did you think? No, you wouldn't have seen it of course.

DENIS: No, I was in here. Reading.

MADAME MENARD: Reading? He reads while he works, does he? That'll make the customers feel welcome.

PHILIPPE turns back to HENRI again.

PHILIPPE: So…what did you reckon? Really.

HENRI: You stuttered.

PHILIPPE: You said that! Besides that?

HENRI: Uh… I don't know, I didn't see anything else. Apart from the bow-tie obviously.

PHILIPPE: Great! So nobody saw anything else!

YOLANDE: Oh yes, I did. You had a little too much make-up on. Like I mentioned.

HENRI: That's right, too much make-up, I remember now!

PHILIPPE looks at HENRI and then at the others. He puts his bow-tie away.

MADAME MENARD: (*To HENRI.*) Enjoying ourselves, are we?

HENRI: He keeps asking so we're going to keep coming up with things, aren't we? The more you look, the more you find, right?

MADAME MENARD: Trust me, Philippe. I watched it extremely carefully and you have absolutely nothing to apologise for. The whole thing was over in two minutes and you smiled the entire time. You came across as very, very...nice.

HENRI: Would anyone like a drink?

Nobody notices HENRI. PHILIPPE sits as YOLANDE tries to comfort him. MADAME MENARD is looking at BETTY.

MADAME MENARD: You look very pale, dear, have you not been eating properly?

BETTY: Yeah, yeah.

YOLANDE: (*To PHILIPPE.*) You're still anxious about it, aren't you?

PHILIPPE: (*Aggressive.*) What? No I'm not anxious about it.

HENRI: Who wants a drink then?

But the others ignore him still.

MADAME MENARD: You're not sleeping well either, are you? You've got these... (*Bags.*)

BETTY: Give it a rest, Mum, I'm fine.

MADAME MENARD: Well if *I* don't ask, who's going to?

HENRI: DOES ANYBODY WANT ANYTHING TO DRINK???

They all look round startled.

PHILIPPE: Jesus, what are you screaming for??

MADAME MENARD: Henri, honestly, you scared the living daylights out of me. Idiot boy.

HENRI: I asked three times! Nobody answered.

PHILIPPE: So what? We didn't hear you, did we? That's why nobody answered, 'cos nobody heard you. No thank you, we don't want a drink.

MADAME MENARD: There's hardly time anyway, we really should be off. But Arlette's not quite ready yet obviously.

HENRI wanders back to the bar where DENIS is clearing up.

HENRI: Denis, uh…go upstairs and see if…if Arlette's back. Just knock on her door and tell her we're…we're all waiting. If she's there.

DENIS: What shall I say if she isn't there? (*HENRI looks.*) Just kidding, boss.

DENIS goes through the door that leads upstairs.

MADAME MENARD: That chap gets away with murder.

PHILIPPE: Look, Riri's got his little Friday jumper on.

HENRI looks at him. BETTY and PHILIPPE share a giggle.

MADAME MENARD: He reads books. He makes jokes. Does he actually *do* anything? And he gets free board and lodging. I mean, the man lives like a king here. Has he any idea how lucky he is? To have you as his…'boss'. Huh. 'Boss'. You. I can't bear to see him make fun of you like that.

HENRI: He doesn't get free board and lodging, he pays rent!

PHILIPPE: Rent, huh! I don't want to state the obvious but you could get twice what you charge him.

HENRI: It's only one room –

PHILIPPE: It's two rooms! Knocked into one. You could get three thousand for a flat that size. You're giving it away at fifteen hundred.

MADAME MENARD: Doesn't bear thinking about what you could do with that extra fifteen hundred every month.

PHILIPPE: Exactly!

HENRI: Yeah, yeah, yeah, I know, I know. I could do the place up. I know!

MADAME MENARD: (*Loud.*) If you know, why don't you do it?!

They all look at her. MADAME MENARD's sudden aggression takes them aback a little.

Of course you don't do it, what am I saying? I look at you and I see your father. Unfortunately. Not once did he ever redecorate this bar. He could have made it very nice if he'd wanted to. Somewhere cosy. Somewhere people'd want to come back to. But…

They've all heard this a hundred times before.

PHILIPPE: (*Weary.*) Why don't you tell us about your dream of an English-type pub, Mum?

HENRI: (*More weary.*) Why not?

MADAME MENARD: That's right, I did dream of us opening a nice 'pub'. Somewhere comfy…but smart too. Keep out the… But that required a little ambition… Huh, ambition. Your father didn't know the meaning of the word. This bar…this…place…*this* was the extent of his ambition.

HENRI: We all know what you thought of Dad! He knew too, don't worry! You never stopped telling him. A word here, a look there. Oh he knew alright. And if he wasn't dead you'd still be telling him! But d'you want to know something? I'm proud of Dad. I'm proud to be just like him!

BETTY: What the hell's this got to do with Dad? We're talking about giving the place a lick of paint, Henri, that's all. You could just try a little harder, you know?

DENIS returns. HENRI turns to him.

DENIS: She's…she's not up there.

HENRI doesn't reply. He goes over to the entrance and looks down the street. MADAME MENARD watches him.

PHILIPPE: Oh God. We're going to be late. We're not late yet but…

The others sit there for a few moments. YOLANDE nervously picks lint from her cardigan. PHILIPPE fidgets impatiently. MADAME MENARD wears a slightly pained expression. BETTY lights another cigarette. The sound of a train passing nearby. After a while

BETTY: Well I'm going to have a drink.

She goes to the bar.

A Suze for me please, Denis. Yolande. It's your night, come and get arseholed with me.

YOLANDE goes over to her, laughing.

YOLANDE: No, don't be daft!

BETTY: Two Suzes.

YOLANDE: No! Stop it, Betty, I mustn't.

YOLANDE giggles slightly as she settles on a bar stool next to BETTY who indicates two drinks to DENIS.

MADAME MENARD: I don't want to appear nosy, Henri, but what *can* your wife be doing at this hour?

HENRI: How should I know? Ask her yourself when she gets here.

MADAME MENARD: Are you angry with me for any reason?

HENRI: No, Mum, not at all. Listen, why don't you go and sit in there for five minutes until she gets here? Denis can bring you something through. I've still got to clean up here anyway.

PHILIPPE: (*To MADAME MENARD.*) Come on, we'll go through while they clean up.

BETTY: (*To DENIS.*) Will you bring the drinks?

YOLANDE: I have to be careful, Betty! Takes nothing to get me tipsy.

MADAME MENARD: (*Quietly to PHILIPPE.*) Can we get off soon and have this wretched birthday dinner? (*He nods.*)

YOLANDE: (*To BETTY.*) Okay, just one then.

MADAME MENARD goes through to the 'restaurant' part with BETTY and YOLANDE. DENIS pours the drinks. HENRI goes back to the entrance and looks out into the street. PHILIPPE joins him. DENIS takes the drinks through to the others.

PHILIPPE: So...everything okay, Riri?

HENRI: Yeah, yeah, fine. Why? What's the matter?

PHILIPPE: Nothing's the matter, I just wondered if everything was alright, that's all.

HENRI: Yeah, well you sound just like a doctor. 'Everything okay?' – like you're expecting the worst or something –

PHILIPPE: For God's sake, I was just asking how you were!

The phone rings. HENRI looks at PHILIPPE momentarily before going to answer it. PHILIPPE goes off to join the others. DENIS returns during HENRI's phone call.

HENRI: (*Into phone.*) *Au Père Tranquille.* Christ, where the hell are you? Have you got any idea what the time is? Yeah. Yeah. What? What're you talking about? What d'you mean you had to go to Monique's to think things over? Why can't you think things over here? What have you got to think over anyway? What? That I'm what? That I do *what?* Who put these bloody idiot ideas into your head?? Arlette, for Christ's sake! You can't walk out on me, it's Friday!! Fridays are for family! (*Calms a little.*) Listen, listen to me, I've got a suggestion. Come back home tonight and you can start this thinking things over business in the morning. Yeah? (*Explodes.*) Fine, take the whole week! Take two weeks! Take the rest of your fucking life!! (*Pause.*) What? 'Cos that's how I talk, that's why!!

HENRI slams the phone down. DENIS stands there.

Know what she said? 'Don't overreact' 'Calm down' she said. Right. No problem. I'll just calmly go over there and smack her in the face.

DENIS: That'll win her round.

HENRI: What's all this 'thinking things over' bollocks? Think what over? And what am I supposed to tell them when they ask why she's still not here?

HENRI fumes for a moment. DENIS looks on sympathetically.

She's got someone else.

DENIS: No. No way.

HENRI: Well what then? Do you think I'm – what did she say? – 'inconsiderate'?

DENIS: Well...

HENRI: She says I'm inconsiderate. D'you think I am? I don't even know what it means.

DENIS: I don't know.

HENRI: See! Tah!

HENRI feels momentarily vindicated.

DENIS: Maybe she means...you treat her badly.

HENRI: 'Treat her badly'!! Do you think I treat her badly??

DENIS: Not me! Her!

HENRI: I treat her fine!! 'Treat her badly'. Fuck. How can I treat her badly? I never even see her! I work thirteen hours a day, I sleep, I eat – that's it! That's all there is. 'Treat her badly'.

HENRI goes back to the window. He's upset.

(*Quietly.*) I can't take much more. I'm sick of it. Sick of it.

DENIS is quite moved.

DENIS: She'll be back.

HENRI: Yeah, yeah.

DENIS: She's just, y'know, thinking things over.

HENRI: Yeah, yeah.

DENIS: Thinking does you good sometimes.

HENRI: No it doesn't.

DENIS: She's just taking a breather that's all. Putting things into perspective, y'know? Weighing up the pros and cons.

HENRI: Splitting fucking hairs. That's all that is.

DENIS: Okay, to you –

HENRI: You pick at things you find things wrong, right? Like with this TV programme. I mean, Jesus, the bow-tie was wrong, who gives a fuck? What do they say when you get married? (*DENIS looks.*) The Mayor, what does he say?

DENIS: 'I now pronounce you man and wife'.

HENRI: Before that!

DENIS: I dunno…'dearly beloved, we are gathered –'

HENRI: Don't be such a prick. 'For better, for worse', right? That's what he says. 'For better, for worse'. So what's there to think about? If it's 'better', fine, if it's 'worse', you just sit it out – till it gets better! That's life. Right? Jesus. She knows what I'm like. She can't expect me to change, can she? I can't change.

DENIS: Why not?

HENRI: Because I'm me, that's why not. You can't change who you are.

DENIS: I don't agree, if you decide –

HENRI: People don't change!

DENIS: D'you want my opinion or not??

HENRI: No!

HENRI goes into the kitchen. DENIS shakes his head. HENRI reappears.

Do you want me to do the duck?

DENIS: Wouldn't you prefer to do the fish?

HENRI: The fish is finished.

DENIS: Yeah, fine, the duck then.

HENRI goes back into the kitchen. DENIS picks up his book and starts reading. YOLANDE comes in with two empty glasses. DENIS looks up.

YOLANDE: May I have two more Suzes, please?

HENRI reappears from the kitchen.

HENRI: Potatoes or green beans?

DENIS: Potatoes.

HENRI disappears again. DENIS closes the book to pour the drinks.

YOLANDE: Did I interrupt your reading?

DENIS shakes his head.

I don't know how you do it. Reading sends me to sleep.

DENIS: Two Suzes. Coming up.

YOLANDE: One's for Betty and one's for me. Ooh, it's cold in here. Don't you think it's cold in here? Betty says another Suze will warm me up.

DENIS: She should know. Here. Happy Birthday. It is your birthday, isn't it?

YOLANDE blushes slightly.

YOLANDE: Yes.

She goes to the dog and leans over it.

Caruso. Caruso. Nothing. Why's he called Caruso?

DENIS: He used to sing. Before he got paralysed. He was a tenor...so the boss called him Caruso. After his favourite singer.

YOLANDE: This dog? He used to sing?

DENIS: Yeah. Like this.

DENIS mimics a dog howling. YOLANDE is surprised.

Whatever came into his head, y'know? But then when he got arthritis...he just stopped. Depressed, I s'pose. After that – not a note. But dogs aren't supposed to sing anyway so...

YOLANDE: (*Compassionately.*) No but they're supposed to move about a bit. Caruso just lies on his tummy all day. Not doing anything. Must be unbearable.

DENIS: Maybe not all day but...

YOLANDE: (*Whispers.*) Do you think he knows he's paralysed?

DENIS: He probably realises when he tries to move.

DENIS mimics the dog trying to move and grunting.

YOLANDE: But what's the point of keeping a paralysed dog?

DENIS: Decoration? Kind of rug. Only alive.

YOLANDE: Oh. I see.

DENIS goes back behind the bar and finishes pouring the drinks. BETTY comes in.

BETTY: Well I've completely blown it. I should never have told Philippe he stuttered, now he's wracked with self-doubt. And Mum's still going on about that fucking horrible bow-tie. Why didn't we just say he was great and leave it at that? This mine?

BETTY takes the drink.

YOLANDE: But I did tell him he was very good.

BETTY: Well who'd have guessed it meant so much to him?

YOLANDE: No it was very important, Betty, you've no idea. They chose *him* to represent the company and he's only number four. Philippe's only number four. I know everybody says he runs the place but he's actually only number four.

BETTY: I know. I work there.

YOLANDE: And we had a holiday booked. For over a year. But we had to cancel it. That's how important this was. Ten days on our own. Relaxing. Without the children for once. Now…

BETTY: I never asked, how are the kids? I haven't seen them in ages.

YOLANDE: Don't talk to me about those children. Michel's fine – as always – but Kevin…don't ask… He lives to get on my nerves. D'you know what he decided to do on Tuesday? Get an ear infection.

MADAME MENARD appears. At that moment HENRI appears from the kitchen with a plate.

HENRI: Denis. Your duck.

DENIS: Thanks, boss.

DENIS collects his dinner and HENRI disappears. DENIS sits at a table. MADAME MENARD looks on in disbelief.

MADAME MENARD: Well. (*DENIS looks up.*) My son would like a tomato juice.

DENIS: One tomato juice. Coming right up.

DENIS gets up and goes behind the bar.

MADAME MENARD: (*To YOLANDE.*) As Arlette hasn't deigned to make an appearance yet. (*To BETTY.*) Should that be hanging out?

BETTY: Should what be hanging out?

MADAME MENARD: (*Looks at BETTY's shirt.*) Is that deliberate or…?

BETTY: Does it worry you?

MADAME MENARD: No, no, it's the fashion I suppose. So…when do we get to meet this famous boyfriend of yours?

BETTY: What boyfriend?

She seems a little uncomfortable. DENIS was about to take the tomato juice through to PHILIPPE but hangs around.

MADAME MENARD: The young man you mentioned.

BETTY: The young man I mentioned?

DENIS smiles to himself. BETTY avoids his look.

MADAME MENARD: Oh don't be so bashful. Nothing wrong with him, is there? I'm only asking, sweetheart, because you made him out to be…well, something special. None of my business I know but I was only thinking this afternoon how nice it would be for you to have someone in your life. After all, Betty…you're thirty years old. I'm sorry but I worry. I do.

DENIS smiles to himself as he wanders off. YOLANDE looks at BETTY in total surprise.

YOLANDE: You're thirty???

BETTY: That's right, Yolande. I'm thirty. And last year when I was twenty-nine you were just as surprised.

YOLANDE: No. Was I?

BETTY: Yes, you were. My mother said she was worried because I was twenty nine already and you went 'You're twenty-nine???'

YOLANDE: Well…if you say so.

MADAME MENARD: By the time I was your age I'd had all three of my children.

YOLANDE: Me too. I mean all two of them.

DENIS returns but stops when he realises the tension.

BETTY: Yes, I know, I'm behind. I'm breaking the rules, throw me in prison, why don't you? Jesus, what else can I say? It fucks me off having to be normal.

BETTY is standing near the table where DENIS's food is. DENIS sits down. They look at each other briefly and he carries on eating.

MADAME MENARD: (*To YOLANDE.*) I'm not finding fault with her. I'm her mother, I'm just worried about her. I mean is that a crime?

YOLANDE nods in agreement. MADAME MENARD stares at DENIS eating. She shakes her head.

We wait. And he eats. God, I'm famished.

She looks at DENIS eating. HENRI comes in from the kitchen with a bowl for the dog.

HENRI: Din dins.

MADAME MENARD: Even the dog.

HENRI: (*To the dog.*) Only ducky duck, that's all I've got. You eat it all up like a good boy.

HENRI goes back into the kitchen as MADAME MENARD wanders over to the dog.

MADAME MENARD: Yummy yummy yummy. Ducky in your tummy. Yes, yes, yes. Yes, yes, yes. *Bon appetit,* sweetiepiedle.

DENIS: Thanks.

MADAME MENARD straightens and glares at DENIS.

MADAME MENARD: Quite the comedian, aren't we?

DENIS shrugs and smiles at her. He takes another mouthful of duck. BETTY smiles to herself. PHILIPPE comes in purposefully.

PHILIPPE: I've decided. I'm going to call Michaud.

He looks round for some encouragement but no one reacts. He goes to the phone and dials. YOLANDE sits next to BETTY.

YOLANDE: Did I say something wrong?

BETTY: (*Friendly.*) No, forget it, 's okay.

PHILIPPE turns back to the room.

PHILIPPE: Michaud always speaks his mind. If there was something wrong with the programme, he'll…y'know?

YOLANDE: I spoke my mind with you, sweetheart –

He gestures for her to be quiet.

PHILIPPE: (*Into phone.*) Michaud, it's Menard, how are you? Can you talk? Listen, did you catch it? Yeah, what did you think? No, of course you can be honest. Yeah, yeah, shoot.

YOLANDE: (*To BETTY.*) What number's Michaud in the firm?

BETTY: Five.

MADAME MENARD: That's below Philippe.

YOLANDE: Of course it is. Philippe's number four.

MADAME MENARD: That's what I said.

PHILIPPE: (*Into phone.*) Yeah well he kept cutting me off, didn't he? …I know the reporter's the star of the show but… Yeah, exactly… Yes, you already said that… What else? …I smiled too much? How can you smile too much? Oh right, right, I see what you're getting at… No, of course not, why would I be angry with you? …Fine, I'll – I'll let you go. Yup. See you Monday.

He hangs up.

MADAME MENARD: That wasn't a very good idea, was it, Philippe? I don't know why you can't just take my word for it. You were very good and there's absolutely nothing wrong with smiling.

PHILIPPE: That's what I just said. 'How can you smile too much?'

MADAME MENARD: But…if you insist on a second opinion, why don't you call your boss? It's what your superiors think that counts. They're the ones who judge you.

PHILIPPE: No, no, I can't bother him with this, it's…it's… I could try Benito…perhaps.

YOLANDE: He's number three.

PHILIPPE looks across to YOLANDE and BETTY.

PHILIPPE: What d'you think?

YOLANDE: Well, why not?

PHILIPPE: I meant Betty.

YOLANDE: Oh, sorry.

MADAME MENARD: 'Benito'? Do I know him?

BETTY: He's a complete arsehole.

MADAME MENARD: Betty, please –

BETTY: I'm sorry but he is. Listen, Philippe, there's something I've been meaning to tell you –

PHILIPPE: (*To MADAME MENARD.*) It's Mazzolini. In the office we call him 'Benito'. Get it? Benito – Mazzolini. Mazzolini – Mussolini.

YOLANDE: Oh! I get it now!

MADAME MENARD: He's that bad?

PHILIPPE: Are you kidding? Mazzolini's a real – so-and-so.
You've no idea how he treats people. How he talks to the
staff! 'Course nobody answers back, everyone's too
scared. They just keep their mouths shut, much safer.

BETTY: That's right. Only this afternoon… I didn't keep
my mouth shut exactly.

*The others look at her. PHILIPPE particularly. HENRI
comes in.*

HENRI: Listen, uh… I just spoke to Arlette. And she's –
she's going to be a while…twenty minutes maybe so…so
why don't you all go on ahead and I'll…y'know? …I'll
meet you there. (*No reply.*) Well?

PHILIPPE: (*To BETTY.*) This afternoon? At the office?

BETTY: Well yeah. I was, y'know, I was dead tired and
I just wasn't in the mood for it. He came in and started
screaming at me as usual and…and… I couldn't help it…
I exploded. I said 'You may be the boss but you've
got no right to talk to people like that'. 'Talk to me
properly!' I wouldn't back down. He was…he was quite
taken aback.

PHILIPPE is stunned but not displeased.

PHILIPPE: You said all that to his face?? I wish I was
there. Wow.

HENRI: Look, Arlette just called and –

PHILIPPE: 'You've got no right…', is that what you said?

BETTY smiles and shrugs.

Wow… I bet he was surprised.

HENRI: ARLETTE'S GOING TO BE TWENTY MINUTES LATE!

The others all turn to him.

MADAME MENARD: Henri, not again!

PHILIPPE: Take it easy, will you!?

MADAME MENARD: What is all this shouting in aid of??

BETTY: (*To HENRI.*) What did she say?

HENRI: She…she's with a friend, y'know? She didn't realise the time.

MADAME MENARD: 'With a friend'. While we starve.

HENRI: She's going to be late…fifteen – twenty minutes at least so…you all go ahead, I'll…we'll meet you there.

MADAME MENARD: Did you tell her we've been waiting half an hour, nearer forty minutes?

HENRI: Yes of course I told her! More than once!

Another hiatus. YOLANDE pulls her cardigan tighter around her.

YOLANDE: Is there a door open somewhere?

PHILIPPE: Give it a rest, will you?! It's hot in here!

MADAME MENARD: Does she expect us to wait till midnight before we toast poor Yoyo's birthday?

HENRI: Exactly! Go on ahead! I'll meet you there, that's what I'm saying. And start without me, okay?

The others look at him.

Look, I prefer you didn't wait for me!

PHILIPPE: What's the matter with you, Riri? What's the problem?

HENRI: There's no problem! And don't call me 'Riri'! I've been asking you for thirty years not to call me 'Riri'! D'you do it just to piss me off or what?!

PHILIPPE: I'm sorry, it just slipped out!

HENRI: Do I call you 'Fifi' all the time?? 'Fifi, Fifi'. No, I bloody well don't!

PHILIPPE: You're fairly wound up for someone without a problem!

MADAME MENARD: Boys, boys! It's Yoyo's birthday and you boys shouldn't fight. So we'll just collect our things and go on ahead. Yoyo, come and fetch your coat.

MADAME MENARD and YOLANDE go into the 'restaurant' to collect their things. HENRI goes back into the kitchen. PHILIPPE turns to BETTY.

PHILIPPE: Listen, uh…you didn't get too carried away, did you? At the office.

BETTY: Well no, not especially.

PHILIPPE: 'Cos you can be pretty…y'know…

BETTY: Not especially.

PHILIPPE: Wow.

PHLIPPE chuckles, slightly reassured, as he wanders off to collect his coat. BETTY's about to follow him but DENIS steps nearer to her.

DENIS: Uh, Betty. Can I say something?

BETTY: Sure.

DENIS: What your mother was saying…y'know? About your 'boyfriend'. I was…really touched.

He puts his arm around her.

BETTY: Yeah? Why?

DENIS: I didn't know I meant so much to you.

BETTY: Yeah except we weren't, y'know, we weren't talking about you.

DENIS: You weren't?

BETTY shakes her head. DENIS takes his arm away.

I feel a complete prat.

BETTY: You just made a mistake, that's all.

DENIS feels a fool. He goes behind the bar and starts to polish the brass beer pump. PHILIPPE and MADAME MENARD appear.

MADAME MENARD: (*Quietly.*) ...Betty didn't go too far with – what d'you call him? Hitler.

PHILIPPE: (*Quietly.*) No, no, it was great what she did, he deserved it.

MADAME MENARD: (*Quietly.*) 'Cos she can be pretty... hardly needs saying.

PHILIPPE: I know, I know but it's okay.

PHILIPPE stops and looks back.

Yolande, what are you doing??

YOLANDE: (*Off.*) I dropped an earring.

PHILIPPE: How can you drop an earring?? (*To MADAME MENARD.*) How can she have dropped an earring?

PHILIPPE goes off again, followed by MADAME MENARD, weary. DENIS is hovering still.

DENIS: Do I...know him?

BETTY: You may have seen him. About.

DENIS: So...you've been seeing him as well as...

BETTY: Uh uh.

HENRI appears from the kitchen. He's surprised to see BETTY still here.

HENRI: What the hell are you still doing here? Are you going or not?

BETTY: Yes, in a minute! Jesus, what's the matter with you this evening??

HENRI: (*To DENIS.*) You've spent an hour polishing that pump! And look at this counter – it's disgusting.

DENIS: I polished the counter ages ago! But I've been serving your family, haven't I? Your brother, your sister, your sister-in-law, your mother, that's a lot of glass marks and fingerprints!

HENRI: Then just do it again! I'm not having customers come in tomorrow to a disgusting counter! What do I say to them, eh? 'Well it *used* to be clean!'. People see a dirty bar and they don't come back, Denis. Do we have customers to spare? You're a lazy bastard!

DENIS: I'll polish the counter again. Don't get so worked up.

HENRI: You've really got it made here, you know that?

DENIS: Well that's debatable…

HENRI: You want to 'debate' it?

DENIS: No, no, it's fine. It's okay.

HENRI: Seriously. Got it made.

HENRI goes back into the kitchen. DENIS shakes his head.

BETTY: He's going mad.

DENIS: He's depressed, that's all. He's had some bad news.

BETTY: Yeah? What?

DENIS: Well he heard something…which…made him…you know…

BETTY: Yeah, bad news, I get it. What?

DENIS: Well…

BETTY: Denis, he's my brother, come on!

DENIS: Arlette's left him.

BETTY: What??

DENIS: No, no, for a week, that's all. To…to think things over.

BETTY: I don't believe it. Fuck. Why?

DENIS: Well…

BETTY: So why?

DENIS: I don't know the whole story…

BETTY: Well tell me what you do know!

DENIS: She says he's…inconsiderate.

PHILIPPE, MADAME MENARD and YOLANDE come in with their coats on. YOLANDE is putting her earring back on.

PHILIPPE: (*To YOLANDE.*) …Don't be stupid! I spend two thousand francs a week at the Duc de Bretagne, we can be twenty minutes late!

They stop by the door.

MADAME MENARD: (*To BETTY.*) Aren't you coming?

BETTY: No, I'm staying for a bit.

PHILIPPE: You're staying?

BETTY: Just to be with Henri for a while, that's all. You go on.

44

PHILIPPE: What for?

BETTY: He's got a little problem.

MADAME MENARD: (*Worried.*) What sort of problem? And how can you help?

BETTY: Well…

PHILIPPE: Come on. Go on, what's wrong with him?

BETTY: Arlette's left him.

MADAME MENARD: What??

DENIS: Only for a week, that's all. To think things over.

MADAME MENARD stares at DENIS.

MADAME MENARD: And how come *you* know??

DENIS: She phoned up… I couldn't help overhearing.

They all take it in. MADAME MENARD sits.

MADAME MENARD: Oh dear. Well… I'm not surprised.

PHILIPPE: It's only for a week he says…it's not the end of the world…maybe she'll come back.

MADAME MENARD: Awful to say I know but…it was inevitable. Things like this always happen to Henri.

YOLANDE: (*Tearful.*) It's terrible for the children. (*The others look.*) It's lucky they haven't got any.

PHILIPPE: So…what are we going to do? We've got to decide. Do I phone up and cancel or…

YOLANDE feels the cold again.

YOLANDE: Close the door, sweetheart, would you?

PHILIPPE is holding the open door. He closes it.

PHILIPPE: Fine. Any offers? Yoyo. It's your birthday – you decide. What would *you* like to do? I go to restaurants all the time so I don't care one way or the other. Your birthday, your decision. Mother's starving and we're half an hour late already but we can easily cancel and go without dinner. So...what would make you happy?

YOLANDE thinks carefully. PHILIPPE taps his foot in frustration. But YOLANDE isn't one to be rushed.

DENIS: I get the feeling...he would rather be left alone this evening.

MADAME MENARD: Oh do you?

HENRI suddenly appears from the kitchen. He's surprised to see them all still here. They all look a him.

HENRI: HOW MUCH LONGER ARE YOU ALL GOING TO STAND AROUND ARGUING FOR??

They all just look back at him.

What? WHAT??

End of Act One.

ACT TWO

About an hour later. The family, except PHILIPPE, is sitting around one of the tables, with the leftovers of a simple meal. The whole place is dark. DENIS stands nearby. No one says anything. After a few moments, PHILIPPE comes in from the kitchen with a tiny improvised birthday cake, a small maltloaf or some such, with half a dozen candles on it. He starts to sing 'Happy Birthday' and the others join in (but not DENIS). PHILIPPE puts the cake in front of YOLANDE and sits next to her. They finish the song.

PHILIPPE: Blow them out, come on.

She blows out the candles and the others applaud. DENIS turns the lights back on. He then goes to the jukebox to resume trying to fix it.

BETTY: Can I open the champagne yet, birthday oberführer?

PHILIPPE: Come on, I didn't say you couldn't open it. I just asked you to wait till she's blown the candles out. I'm sorry but there's a right way of doing things.

BETTY opens the champagne but PHILIPPE takes the bottle and starts pouring.

YOLANDE: Pity there isn't any music.

She turns towards DENIS.

Isn't it working yet?

DENIS: I'm getting there…

PHILIPPE: Henri, hand me your glass.

HENRI is sitting glumly at the end of the table.

Come on, have a drink, what harm can it do?

HENRI pushes his glass towards PHILIPPE.

47

MADAME MENARD: Oh do cheer up, Henri. You're not going to sulk the whole evening, are you? A smile? For Mummy?

HENRI doesn't respond.

She couldn't take any more so she's having a week off. You're not such a barrel of laughs at the best of times. Women need a breather every now and again.

PHILIPPE: (*To BETTY.*) Y'know, what's worrying me… it's Benito…he was very strange on the phone just now.

YOLANDE: You've got to call him back in a minute.

PHILIPPE: I know I've got to call him back in a minute. He said in half an hour. And it hasn't been half an hour yet, has it? (*To BETTY.*) He was very curt with me – 'I can't talk now'.

YOLANDE: You said.

BETTY: Well he's never exactly warm.

PHILIPPE: Yeah I know, I know but he was particularly unfriendly. That's what's worrying me. (*Weary.*) I'm sick of the whole business. I'm supposed to be on holiday.

HENRI: (*Suddenly remembering.*) I had this dream last night. We were all there, all of us. Sitting round this big table. And there was this enormous fish…in my hand. And I was hitting Mum over the head with it.

The others look at him. Especially MADAME MENARD.

MADAME MENARD: (*Suddenly.*) A fish??

HENRI: (*Glum again.*) Uh uh.

MADAME MENARD: But that's good luck! A fish means money! You're going to be rich, Henri!

HENRI: (*Uninterested.*) Yeah?

PHILIPPE puts his present for YOLANDE on the table with the other small pile of presents. YOLANDE picks it up.

YOLANDE: Can I open them now?

PHILIPPE: What they're there for.

YOLANDE is about to open it.

MADAME MENARD: Wait, wait. Start with this one. It's from me. You'll see why in a moment. And this one here's Henri's, his comes second. You'll see.

MADAME MENARD indicates the first two presents. YOLANDE gingerly opens MADAME MENARD's present which is little more than a card. YOLANDE looks at it.

YOLANDE: Oh. What is it?

PHILIPPE: Well you can see what it is, sweetheart.

YOLANDE: It's a photo of a dog.

She looks up.

BETTY: You collecting photos of dogs these days?

YOLANDE: Not really, no. That's why I'm confused.

She looks back at the card.

Oh. There's some sort of…coupon. (*Reads.*) 'This coupon can be –

PHILIPPE, HENRI and MADAME MENARD are all now looking over YOLANDE's shoulders.

PHILIPPE/HENRI/MADAME MENARD: (*All together.*) '– redeemed…'

YOLANDE: '…redeemed…for a dog'.

She looks at MADAME MENARD, PHILIPPE and HENRI who all smile back at her. She reads on.

49

'…at the Lost Pups Kennels, Fifty-seven Boulevard des Parloirs…' (*To MADAME MENARD*.) Are you giving me a dog?

MADAME MENARD: That's him in the photo. His name's Bagpipes.

YOLANDE: What?

PHILIPPE: Bagpipes.

MADAME MENARD: If you don't like it you can change it.

YOLANDE looks.

PHILIPPE: The name she means.

YOLANDE: Oh. Yes.

MADAME MENARD: He's still only a puppy so you're allowed to change it. 'Cos he's not used to it yet.
He won't mind, really.

YOLANDE: No.

MADAME MENARD: He's a boy by the way. You'll have a much easier time with a boy, believe me.

YOLANDE nods. She stares at the photo.

HENRI: But I like the name Bagpipes.

YOLANDE: Erm…thank you…thank you very much, Madame Menard… Does…does it come with…any instructions?

The others look at her. BETTY smiles to herself.

BETTY: You just water it once a day.

PHILIPPE throws BETTY a look and turns back to YOLANDE.

PHILIPPE: You don't seem very pleased. Don't you like him?

MADAME MENARD: Of course she likes him, don't be ridiculous. She's just surprised, that's all.

YOLANDE: That's right! I'm…surprised…but…

MADAME MENARD: Listen, Yoyo, sweetheart. I'm very
experienced with dogs. I've always kept dogs and believe
me once you get to know them you'll be in for a big
surprise. Do you know what I honestly think? From the
bottom of my heart? Dogs…never let you down.

HENRI: That's true. Unfortunately…it's true.

MADAME MENARD: No one ever loved me…like my
Freddy loved me. No one understood me… When he
died…he was only eighteen…when he died, do you know
what I did?

PHILIPPE/HENRI/BETTY: Yeah, yeah, we do.

MADAME MENARD: I moved house.

DENIS: (*To himself.*) Good to remind oneself.

*Only BETTY catches the comment. She smiles at him.
YOLANDE looks at the photo again.*

YOLANDE: It looks like Henri's dog.

PHILIPPE: (*Quietly.*) He's a 'he', not an 'it'.

MADAME MENARD: He's the same breed obviously.
Since my Freddy… I always buy the same breed.

HENRI: Mum gave me him too. The cripple. That's the
only problem with these dogs. After a while they
collapse. But Caruso, he's…so good-natured…he never
complains. But they don't. Isn't that right, Mum?

YOLANDE: (*To MADAME MENARD.*) Was yours…paralysed
as well?

MADAME MENARD: Of course.

YOLANDE looks at the photo and begins to cry softly.

She's such a sensitive thing.

YOLANDE puts on a brave face. MADAME MENARD hands her the second present.

Henri's.

YOLANDE opens it and takes out the present – a dog-lead.

HENRI: It's a dog-lead.

MADAME MENARD: See?

YOLANDE: A dog-lead. To go with…

HENRI: See those studs? They're silver-plated. Silver-plated studs.

YOLANDE: (*Holding back tears.*) How nice. Thank you.

YOLANDE carefully puts the lead back into its box as PHILIPPE ostentatiously puts his present in front of her.

PHILIPPE: And this…is from me.

YOLANDE starts to cry again.

That's enough being sensitive I think, Yoyo.

YOLANDE: Sorry. I'm… I'm not used to drinking so much, that's all.

She puts on a brave face and opens PHILIPPE's present. She looks in.

Oh. Another dog-lead.

She takes a 'choker' out of its box.

PHILIPPE: It's not a lead. It's a choker, sweetheart.

YOLANDE: Ah! Are these diamonds?

PHILIPPE just smiles benignly.

But it's…it's far too expensive for a dog.

PHILIPPE: It's for you! It's not for Bagpipes, it's for you! It's not a dog collar, it's a woman's choker!

HENRI: Yeah, it's a choker.

YOLANDE: (*Relieved.*) Oh thank you, thank you, Philippe. I'm going to try it on right away!

PHILIPPE stands behind her and puts the choker on her. A black velvet choker set with diamonds.

Does it suit me?

MADAME MENARD: Very nice.

BETTY: Now try barking.

MADAME MENARD throws BETTY a look.

MADAME MENARD: (*To YOLANDE.*) It's beautiful, it's... (*To BETTY.*) It's very stylish.

PHILIPPE: Happy Birthday, my darling.

He kisses her.

MADAME MENARD: Oh he's so sweet. Wait, wait, do it again, do it again!

MADAME MENARD produces a cheap camera from her bag. PHILIPPE goes through the motion of kissing YOLANDE again but bored already by it. He sits.

(*To YOLANDE.*) You are so lucky, Yoyo. To have such a sweet husband. A husband who cares, that's a godsend.

HENRI: (*Suddenly.*) Comes down to money, that's all! Did you expect Dad to do that, did you? Buy you diamonds on the HP? 'A husband who cares'. Shit. That's easy for you to say.

MADAME MENARD: For heaven's sake, Henri, what's got into you? Who's talking about your father? We all know you're sad this evening but it's hardly my fault your wife can't stand the sight of you! Now pull yourself together! Please!

HENRI: I said I wanted to be alone, didn't I? But you all insisted on staying, I didn't ask you all to stay!

MADAME MENARD: We could hardly have left you here on your own, could we? We're not completely unfeeling. Don't you think we'd have rather gone to the restaurant?? I mean the duck was alright...

PHILIPPE: (*Standing.*) Fine!! Right! Now we're going to toast Yoyo's birthday. If nobody minds, that is. Henri. Your glass.

PHILIPPE holds up HENRI's glass and he takes it. YOLANDE looks across to DENIS.

I give you –

YOLANDE: What about him? Doesn't he get a drink?

PHILIPPE: Yeah. Sure. Why not?

DENIS comes over and PHILIPPE pours him a glass and hands it to him.

I give you –

DENIS: Thank you, Madame Menard.

YOLANDE: Don't mention it.

PHILIPPE: (*Overlapping.*) Don't mention it. I give you – Yoyo.

ALL: Yoyo.

PHILIPPE: I've forgotten what I was going to say now.

He throws a look to DENIS.

Oh yes, right. To Yoyo, the mother of my children... who's stood beside me for nine – ten years... Never complaining, always cheerful –

DENIS: Congratulations, Madame Menard.

PHILIPPE throws him an even fiercer look.

PHILIPPE: I haven't finished! Well it's too late now, I've lost my train of thought. Anyway so... Happy Birthday, darling.

He kisses her on the top of the head. And they all take a sip.
Except BETTY who drains her glass.

It's a toast, Betty! You don't just gulp it down!

BETTY: Fucking hell, are we in the army all of a sudden or
what?? What's got into you??

PHILIPPE tries to remain calm. YOLANDE holds up a knife.

YOLANDE: How many slices shall I cut?

PHILIPPE aggressively counts round the table.

PHILIPPE: One two three four five. There's five people.
So that makes five slices.

YOLANDE: They'll be very thin. The cake's so small.

MADAME MENARD: It's a gesture.

YOLANDE slowly counts round the table.

YOLANDE: One two three four five... (*Sees DENIS.*) What
about him? Isn't he having any?

PHILIPPE: Alright. Six then. That cake's ridiculous.

HENRI: What d'you expect? D'you think I keep a fridge
full of birthday cakes just in case?

HENRI sulkily goes back to behind the bar. YOLANDE starts
to cut the cake carefully.

MADAME MENARD: (*To BETTY.*) So...where's your
present for Yoyo?

BETTY just looks at her.

Just teasing.

PHILIPPE: My kid sister wouldn't stoop so low as to give
birthday presents. That'd be far too ordinary.

BETTY: Leave it out, will you?

PHILIPPE: Is it too much to ask you could have bought her a lousy paperback? A gesture that's all. A gesture on Yoyo's birthday.

BETTY: Treat people like shit all year round, then give them some stupid present and everything's okay.

PHILIPPE: Giving nothing's much more radical.

YOLANDE: I love getting presents.

BETTY: Yeah, really? You like your new dog do you?

YOLANDE: No but in general.

MADAME MENARD almost spills her drink.

PHILIPPE: Oh well done, Yoyo, brilliant! Very tactful!

MADAME MENARD: No, no, don't worry, Philippe.

YOLANDE: What? What did I do?

Suddenly the jukebox blurts out music. The same track as at the beginning.

Ah! (*To PHILIPPE.*) D'you want to dance?

PHILIPPE: No, not really.

YOLANDE: Oh go on, just one.

PHILIPPE: I'm too tired!

YOLANDE turns to HENRI who's still behind the bar.

YOLANDE: Henri?

HENRI just shakes his head. YOLANDE is disappointed. But she then proudly feels her new choker. DENIS comes over.

DENIS: Madame Menard?

YOLANDE looks up. She then looks to PHILIPPE.

PHILIPPE: Yeah, go ahead, why not?

DENIS clears a space for some dancing. He and YOLANDE start to jive. DENIS is very good at it and soon YOLANDE is really enjoying herself.

(*To MADAME MENARD.*) I don't know what women see in that sort of dancing.

MADAME MENARD: (*Not hearing.*) What?

PHILIPPE: (*Shout.*) That's not real music!

But DENIS and YOLANDE are having a great time. YOLANDE kicks off her shoes and really gets into it. HENRI wanders off into the kitchen. MADAME MENARD motions to PHILIPPE that the music is so loud and wanders downstairs to the toilets. After a while the music fades and they stop dancing.

YOLANDE: Oh! My shoes!

Slightly giddily YOLANDE retrieves her shoes.

Thank you, Denis, I haven't had so much fun in ages!

PHILIPPE: (*Quietly.*) Doesn't take much to give you fun.

YOLANDE: (*To DENIS.*) You're a fabulous dancer. Did you have lessons?

DENIS: No, no, I just make it up as I go along.

YOLANDE: Well it was really nice, thanks.

DENIS: My birthday present. Hey, do you fancy another one?

But it's PHILIPPE who answers first.

PHILIPPE: No that's fine thank you.

YOLANDE looks disappointed.

DENIS: (*To YOLANDE.*) Sorry. He's the boss.

Suddenly a crash from offstage.

MADAME MENARD: (*Off.*) AAAAH!!

PHILIPPE jumps to his feet.

PHILIPPE: Mum!!

PHILIPPE, YOLANDE and BETTY hurry down the stairs. HENRI appears from the kitchen.

HENRI: What's going on??

DENIS indicates downstairs and HENRI rushes down to the basement. DENIS goes to the top of the stairs and looks down.

(*Off.*) What happened?

PHILIPPE: (*Off.*) What d'you think happened?? She fell down the stairs!

MADAME MENARD: (*Off.*) Oooooooh.

PHILIPPE: (*Off.*) It's too bloody dark!!

HENRI: (*Off.*) Too bloody dark, is that all you can say!?

MADAME MENARD: (*Off.*) Don't fight! I'm dying here!!

But HENRI and PHILIPPE continue to argue indistinctly. DENIS slowly begins to clear up as BETTY appears from downstairs.

DENIS: How is she?

BETTY: Few bruises. Scared mainly. Philippe's having a go at Henri for not changing the lightbulb. He keeps fucking up, doesn't he? Poor Henri.

DENIS: (*Stops.*) Do you think it's too dark on those stairs?

BETTY: Do *I*?

DENIS: Yeah.

BETTY: Not particularly.

DENIS: So why d'you say Henri keeps fucking up?

BETTY's surprised by the question.

I think it's you keeps fucking *him* up. All of you.

BETTY: That's a bit harsh.

DENIS: Yeah, well.

DENIS seems very serious. BETTY looks at him as he takes a pile of dirty plates through to the kitchen. He comes straight back in to collect more stuff. He stops.

Is it the guy who runs the driving school?

BETTY: What?

DENIS: The…'famous boyfriend'. This 'someone special'.

BETTY: Ah! My 'boyfriend'. Yeah, I'd forgotten all about him. No, it's not the guy who runs the driving school.

DENIS: Who is it then? Is he…local?

BETTY: Could say.

PHILIPPE suddenly appears at the top of the stairs and stares fiercely at DENIS.

PHILIPPE: Right! Since my brother is incapable of giving you even the simplest order – I'll do it. First thing in the morning you go out and you buy a hundred watt lightbulb and you install it on that staircase! Have I made myself clear??

PHILIPPE turns and goes back down the stairs.

BETTY: Cheerful tonight, isn't he?

DENIS: Could sweet-talk you into anything, your brother.

DENIS carries on clearing up.

BETTY: (*Chuckles.*) So…you can see me with the guy from the driving school, can you?

DENIS: How about the chemist?

BETTY: The chemist??

DENIS: I'm just…groping in the dark here.

BETTY: Why d'you want to know anyway?

DENIS: Dunno. Curiosity I s'pose.

BETTY smiles to herself as DENIS clears away some more plates. HENRI returns and sits at a table. Defeated.

HENRI: (*To BETTY.*) Take Mum a glass of water down, would you?

BETTY: Everything okay?

HENRI: Yeah, yeah, she'll live.

BETTY: I meant you.

HENRI: Me? Who gives a shit about me?

BETTY looks at him for a moment, not sure what to say. She then gets a glass of water from behind the bar and goes down to the basement. HENRI looks at DENIS who's returned from the kitchen.

I'll finish up on my own.

DENIS: No, no, no, don't be so defeatist, boss. You never know what the future holds. She may well even –

HENRI: What the fuck are you talking about? I meant you go home and I'll finish up here on my own!

DENIS: Ah, right. Listen, I don't mind hanging around, I've got nothing else to do this evening.

HENRI stares into the middle distance.

HENRI: I really thought she'd turn up. I kept thinking she'll realise she can't just, you know…just walk out on me after fifteen years. I mean, we're too used to each other, right?…What a mug. I might as well believe in Father Christmas.

DENIS looks at him.

DENIS: Why don't you go over there? To Monique's.

HENRI: What the fuck for? To make an even bigger arse of myself?

DENIS: I dunno. Talk to her.

HENRI: No way! Fuck. *She* left *me.* If anyone's going to go round to anyone, she's going to come round to me. You want me to get down on my knees and beg? Tah. (*Sighs.*) You've got the right idea, Denis. No wife, no family. No one nagging you all day, 'do this, do that'.

DENIS: No one nagging me… Look, I'm not saying you got to get down on your knees. Just…just tell her you feel bad, y'know? …tell her you miss her, I dunno. Better than just sitting about for a week feeling sorry for yourself. Hey!

DENIS hurriedly fetches his book and rifles through it.

I only read this bit this afternoon. Listen, this is…dead right. This is…really apt. (*Reading.*) 'Profound is our suffering… How rare for two souls to arrive at love in the same way…'

DENIS looks at HENRI.

HENRI: Bollocks.

DENIS closes the book.

I'm not really in the mood for reading right now, okay?

DENIS: So when are you? Never.

HENRI: Yeah well even less at this precise moment.

Silence. BETTY comes back and goes to sit by the bar. HENRI wanders over to the dog.

You don't give a shit, do you? What's your answer? More sleep. (*To DENIS.*) She's the one who left me, right? So why would she want to see me? Tah.

DENIS: Not necessarily. I know, let's ask a woman. Betty, what do you think? If you walked out on someone, you know, as a spur of the moment thing, wouldn't you... wouldn't you want him to show up and...say sorry...that he needs you...that he's scared he'll lose you...?

BETTY looks straight at DENIS.

All that stuff... Wouldn't you like that? Wouldn't it make you...you know...feel better?

BETTY: (*Straight at him.*) I would like that. Yes.

DENIS: Right. (*To HENRI.*) See? She'd like that.

HENRI: Yeah but Betty's... I'm not apologising, alright? My father spent his whole life saying sorry. And look how he ended up!

DENIS: How did he end up?

HENRI: *She* left him! He died of a broken heart.

BETTY: (*To DENIS.*) No he didn't.

HENRI: You're nice – and that's what happens.

BETTY sits nearer to HENRI.

BETTY: How do *you* end up, Henri? (*No reply.*) Arlette's your wife. Not Mum. Arlette wants you to be nice to her. She'd like that, I know she would.

HENRI doesn't reply. MADAME MENARD appears at the top of the stairs with PHILIPPE and YOLANDE.

MADAME MENARD: I'm fine, I'm fine. I had a scare, that's all. I couldn't breathe, I was in shock, I thought my leg was broken but mercifully it's over now, I'm... I'm...

PHILIPPE: You had a terrible fright, Mum.

MADAME MENARD: I know, I know.

YOLANDE: So did we! When I saw you in a crumpled heap at the bottom of the stairs – ooh!

YOLANDE arrives by the bar and looks carefully at all the bottles.

You know… I could do with a little drinky.

PHILIPPE helps MADAME MENARD into a chair but looks across to YOLANDE.

PHILIPPE: Hey, go easy on the drink, will you?

YOLANDE: 'Go easy on the drink'. Like I'm a drunk or something.

PHILIPPE: You've already had one more than you should.

YOLANDE: It's my birthday! I can have a drink, can't I? Or a dance? When was the last time I had a drink?

PHILIPPE: I don't remember.

YOLANDE: Neither do I! See?

PHILIPPE: That's completely beside the point. I'm talking about tonight. Here, now!

BETTY: (*To PHILIPPE.*) You're pissing me right off, you are. Yoyo, here, I'll get you a drink.

BETTY goes behind the bar.

PHILIPPE: Great, Betty, well done. That's just what I'd expect from you!

BETTY: It's her birthday!

YOLANDE: It is.

PHILIPPE: Okay so it's her birthday, how many time do you want to remind us?? What d'you want her to do? Jump up on the table and give us a bit of lap dancing?!

YOLANDE giggles at the thought.

MADAME MENARD: Ah!

PHILIPPE: What??

MADAME MENARD: Your phonecall, sweetheart.
You haven't forgotten, have you?

PHILIPPE: How could I forget? I can't think about
anything else. (*Looks at his watch.*) Ten more minutes.

YOLANDE: I'm not mad.

She pulls her cardigan around her tighter.

There's a door open somewhere. There's a draft…coming
from over there…hitting me right here.

She indicates her neck. BETTY hands her a drink.

Ooh.

*They clink glasses. YOLANDE sips. HENRI springs up out
of his stupor and purposefully puts on his jacket.*

HENRI: I'm off. I'm going out…for a while. I'll be… I'll be
back later. If you want to stay…otherwise… Denis, you'll
lock up, alright?

DENIS nods.

MADAME MENARD: Where on earth are you going?

HENRI: For a walk.

MADAME MENARD: For a walk? Out there? In the
middle of the night?

HENRI: I feel like going for a walk.

MADAME MENARD: Well don't mind us, Henri, will you?
We'll just sit about here. (*Indicates DENIS.*) He'll look after
us, I'm sure. If he's not too busy reading. Or dancing.

HENRI stops by the door.

HENRI: I'm going to see Arlette.

MADAME MENARD: Arlette? Whatever for?

HENRI: To...to talk to her.

MADAME MENARD: What a peculiar idea.

HENRI: Why?

MADAME MENARD: Well what could you possibly say
   to her?

HENRI: Er...I don't know. I'm just going to, y'know?
   ...talk to her. Better than sitting here all week...feeling
   sorry for myself.

   MADAME MENARD sort of sneers at him.

MADAME MENARD: All comes down to character,
   I suppose.

BETTY: What??

MADAME MENARD: Let's just say I couldn't do it.

BETTY: Jesus.

MADAME MENARD: To lower yourself like that...

BETTY: Yeah well I disagree.

PHILIPPE: If he wants to go, let him go!

   *PHILIPPE looks at his watch anxiously. HENRI looks as
   though he's losing his nerve slightly. BETTY gives him an
   encouraging look. He then decides and leaves hurriedly.
   MADAME MENARD turns to BETTY.*

MADAME MENARD: This was your brainwave, I suppose?

BETTY: No.

DENIS: It was mine, Madame Menard, I'm afraid.

MADAME MENARD: Yours? Well it's nothing to brag about.

BETTY: That's your opinion.

MADAME MENARD: D'you know what's going to happen? The exact opposite of what you hope's going to happen. She'll send him packing. Simple as that. She didn't walk out on him only to have him fall back into her arms three hours later. Besides, begging never works, it's very off-putting. And most unattractive.

PHILIPPE: Unfortunately Mum's right. Well you know what they say? 'Flee from me and I'll follow. But follow me – and I'll flee'.

MADAME MENARD: Exactly.

YOLANDE: 'Flee from you – I'll…follow' What?

PHILIPPE: (*Aggressively.*) Flee-from-me-I'll-follow-but-follow-me-I'll-flee!

YOLANDE: Oh. Yes… (*Doubtful.*) Well… (*Unconvinced.*) No…

BETTY: (*To MADAME MENARD.*) Do you know why she left? No you don't. So how can you be so sure?

MADAME MENARD: I don't know the exact reason, no, but it isn't hard to see what's going on. You forget, Betty, I made Henri. I brought him into this world. I know him like only a mother can know a son.

YOLANDE: My Kevin's a complete stranger.

MADAME MENARD shoots a look at YOLANDE before turning back to BETTY.

MADAME MENARD: You'd need the patience of a saint to put up with that man.

PHILIPPE attempts to be conciliatory with BETTY.

PHILIPPE: Do you know why she left?

BETTY: No I don't know why she left. Let's just leave it, shall we?

MADAME MENARD: Nothing ever goes right for Henri. Never has. Nothing any of us can do about it. Since the day he was born, he needed constant attention, you couldn't take your eyes off him for a second. If it wasn't his health it was his tantrums. And he was a late walker. He was a late talker too. He was more or less late at everything. You know, you –

YOLANDE: My Kevin's the same. He's so...slow.

MADAME MENARD: You can tell right from the start how they're going to turn out. Amazing. He was only two days old – I'll never forget this – only two days old and my mother looked at Henri in his cot and she said 'This one's going to be a nightmare'. Imagine! Two days old!

BETTY: 'Whereas Philippe...'

MADAME MENARD: Exactly!

PHILIPPE: Mum, come on, change the record.

MADAME MENARD: I can't help comparing, can I?? I bring both my boys up in exactly the same way and they're like chalk and cheese!

BETTY: We know, Mum, we know! Everybody knows! By some miracle Philippe turns out to be absolutely perfect whereas Henri's a total arsehole!

MADAME MENARD: I'll just stop talking then.

A hiatus.

DENIS: (*To BETTY.*) What about you?

BETTY: What?

DENIS: How did you turn out?

BETTY: I'm a girl. We're graded differently.

YOLANDE looks at them.

YOLANDE: You two are friends, aren't you?

BETTY: What?

YOLANDE: 'Cos you're quite familiar with each other I noticed.

BETTY: Well maybe.

YOLANDE: You are, I'm right.

BETTY shrugs. DENIS wanders off. YOLANDE leans in.

He's a fab dancer.

YOLANDE wanders over to the dog. MADAME MENARD sits in the corner, rubbing her stomach.

MADAME MENARD: I'm having a little difficulty with this duck.

Nobody responds. PHILIPPE looks at his watch anxiously. YOLANDE bends down over the dog.

YOLANDE: It looks dead this dog. And I'm getting one just like it. Oh God.

PHILIPPE glances at MADAME MENARD and then turns to YOLANDE.

PHILIPPE: I did ask you not to drink so much.

YOLANDE: I haven't drunk so much! I've had five small drinks! I'm allowed to say he looks dead, aren't I? He hasn't moved!

PHILIPPE: He never moves!

YOLANDE: But when he's asleep he looks even deader!

PHILIPPE: Alright, fine! You've said it!

YOLANDE: And to think I'm getting one exactly the same…it's awful…that's all there is to it!

PHILIPPE: God, you're such a…

YOLANDE: Such a what?

He turns away from her. After a moment.

Do I pass judgement on you when you arrive home
every Tuesday at three in the morning?

PHILIPPE: Excuse me, Betty – Yoyo – I don't see what
this has got to do with what time I get home from work.
Listen, you're beginning to talk gibberish, I think
perhaps we should –

YOLANDE: It's got to do with the fact that I have a right to
a drink every once in a while…and also that you could
be nicer to me…

She starts to cry quietly. PHILIPPE doesn't respond.

We're supposed to be on holiday…and I end up with a
dog that won't move.

PHLIPPE awkwardly puts his arms around her.

PHILIPPE: Sweetheart.

YOLANDE: No.

She pushes his arm away.

PHILIPPE: My darling.

*He holds her gently. She cries quietly. She leans into him.
She's slightly unsteady on her feet.*

Let's get some fresh air. Come on. Do us both good.

He leads YOLANDE out of the bar.

MADAME MENARD: Such a sweet man.

BETTY: You took the words right out of my mouth.

MADAME MENARD: How was I to know she doesn't like
dogs? (*Pause.*) Would you like Bagpipes?

BETTY looks at her. MADAME MENARD then looks across to DENIS.

How about you? He's paid for.

DENIS gestures that he lives here.

DENIS: I dunno, two crippled dogs under one roof...

MADAME MENARD suddenly checks her watch.

MADAME MENARD: It's time for Philippe to make his phonecall.

BETTY: All this bullshit over two minutes of television. Who gives a shit what that scumbag Benito thought of it anyway?

MADAME MENARD: Betty, really! Where did I go wrong that you grew up swearing like a trooper? Just for once couldn't you try to sound a little ladylike?

BETTY: Fuck 'ladylike'. Being a 'lady' isn't my sole purpose in life.

MADAME MENARD: Let me tell you something, young 'lady', you're wrong. Nobody likes to hear women talk like that. Especially men. Like it or not you're a woman and women are supposed to talk properly. I didn't invent the rules.

DENIS: Well if you don't mind me saying, Madame Menard, but –

MADAME MENARD: And who the hell asked you? This is a private conversation between mother and daughter.

DENIS: Pardon me.

DENIS, pissed off, wanders into the kitchen. MADAME MENARD watches him go.

BETTY: Some things are more shocking than bad language, Mum.

MADAME MENARD: What on earth do you mean by that?

BETTY: You can be crude without using obscene words, that's what I mean.

MADAME MENARD: What are you trying to say, Betty?

BETTY: Haven't you noticed Henri eating his heart out all evening? He's your son. Are you remotely concerned about him? Or is it only Philippe's little problems that interest you?

MADAME MENARD: Betty –

BETTY: Philippe this, Philippe that… He may be wonderful but he treats his wife like shit. You think *I'm* crude? Philippe puts me in the shade. And look at the way you talk to Denis – like he's a dog or something. What am I saying, 'like a dog'? Dogs get treated better in this family than people!

MADAME MENARD: (*Tearful.*) My God, I didn't know I was such a monster.

BETTY: Now I've made you cry. I s'pose that makes me the monster.

YOLANDE comes in from outside. She goes to MADAME MENARD and delivers a reluctant speech, defeated.

YOLANDE: Erm… I didn't mean to hurt your feelings. I'm very sorry…there.

MADAME MENARD: You didn't hurt my feelings. I just assumed as a mother you'd be fond of animals. I'm the one who should say sorry.

MADAME MENARD chokes back a tear. YOLANDE wrongly assumes she's upset because of her.

YOLANDE: No, no, I love animals! I do! It's just that dog over there depresses me.

MADAME MENARD: It doesn't matter, Yoyo.

YOLANDE sits. They all sit there.

(*Anxiously.*) Where's Philippe?

YOLANDE: He's outside. On his mobile. Talking to 'Benito'.

MADAME MENARD: Oh. Thank God.

YOLANDE: He said there was a better signal outside.

But suddenly PHILIPPE comes marching in. Angry. He goes straight up to BETTY.

PHILIPPE: Right! Tell me again what you told me earlier, Yoyo – I mean Betty – what did you tell me?

BETTY: Philippe, for God's sake, calm down will you?

PHILIPPE: I asked you if you got 'carried away' this afternoon. With Benito. 'Not especially'. That's what you said. 'Not especially'!

BETTY: Is this worth having a heart attack over?

PHILIPPE: That's not the way he tells it!! He says your behaviour was totally out of order! He's incensed!! I asked him what he thought of my appearance on television – and he didn't even want to talk about it!

DENIS comes noisily out of the kitchen but quickly senses the atmosphere.

Well?

BETTY: Well what? He's not used to people answering back. He can't take it. What more can I say?

PHILIPPE: Have you any conception of what you've done??

HENRI comes in from the street but stops by the door.

HENRI: She wouldn't talk to me.

But nobody reacts.

MADAME MENARD: So you've no idea what he thought of your TV appearance?

PHILIPPE: None at all! There was only topic of conversation – Betty. Her performance was the big event of the day. Not mine.

He sits in a chair right next to YOLANDE. She immediately taps PHILIPPE on the shoulder but he ignores her.

(*Gestures to BETTY.*) You are this close to getting sacked.

HENRI: I shouted up at the window but she didn't answer.

MADAME MENARD: He'd really sack her?

PHILIPPE: What d'you expect?

YOLANDE taps PHILIPPE again but he still ignores her.

MADAME MENARD: I don't believe it.

PHILIPPE: Well he's hardly going to promote her, is he?

HENRI is about to shout but controls himself.

HENRI: (*Deliberately.*) I woke up the whole street.

They all look round to him.

Arlette wouldn't see me.

MADAME MENARD: What did I tell you?

YOLANDE taps PHILIPPE on the shoulder a third time. He now turns and barks at her.

PHILIPPE: What do you want??

YOLANDE: You're sitting on my cardigan.

PHILIPPE gets up and walks away. HENRI goes to the bar to pour himself a drink. YOLANDE wraps the released cardigan tighter around her.

I'm chilly.

HENRI: (*To BETTY and DENIS.*) Thanks for the advice you two. Terrific.

MADAME MENARD: My God... (*To PHILIPPE.*) And he never even mentioned the show?

PHILIPPE: No!

BETTY: I don't understand, why are you so upset? We both feel the same about him. Benito's a bastard. You've been dying for someone to stand up to him. Did I dream this all up or what?

PHILIPPE stares out the window.

MADAME MENARD: If you spoke to this Mussolini man with anything like your customary delicacy, it's hardly surprising he hit the roof. Philippe recommended you for the job. How could you?

PHILIPPE: How could she?? Easy! You don't expect her to give a flying fart how all this makes me look, do you? Let me tell you something, Betty. When you were a kid and you used to shout your mouth off, it was funny. The family clown, we pissed ourselves. NOT ANY MORE!! You're thirty years old! You're supposed to be a grown up! So why don't you get your brain into fucking gear and give your arsehole a rest!!

BETTY: And I thought you'd 'die laughing'.

PHILIPPE: Die laughing?? 'Cos you insulted the berk who watches over my every move??

BETTY: I didn't really insult him, you know? I spoke my mind. There's a difference.

MADAME MENARD: Why are you so pig-headed, Betty? You were showing off, why don't you just admit it?

BETTY: I wasn't showing off! I told the guy what I thought of him, that's all! But maybe Philippe's changed his mind. Maybe Benito's his new best friend in school, I don't give a bollocks any more!

PHILIPPE: You've fucked up and you've landed me right
in the shit!!

PHILIPPE collapses into a chair, exhausted.

MADAME MENARD: (*To BETTY.*) See what you've done?
Until today your brother was very highly thought of in
that firm. Who'll trust him now?

PHILIPPE: Exactly. Don't bother with Menard, he's the
guy who hires hysterical women.

MADAME MENARD: D'you really think he'd fire her?

PHILIPPE: He as good as told me.

MADAME MENARD: (*To BETTY.*) Do you realise –

BETTY: I don't give a fuck.

PHILIPPE: You don't give a fuck because you'll expect me
to find you another job as per bloody usual.

BETTY: I'm not asking you for anything ever again. Don't
worry!

PHILIPPE: Yeah, yeah. I can already hear it a month from
now. When you're flat broke. 'Oh, Philippe, you don't
happen to know someone who –

BETTY: I won't ask!

PHILIPPE: That'll make a change!

BETTY: Maybe it's time for a change! From here on, don't
do anything for me, alright? No more favours. They cost
too much.

PHILIPPE: No more favours? Fine. Manage by yourself.

BETTY: I will. All on my own. Just like a grown up.

PHILIPPE: I can't wait to see it. All on your own? You?
In six months time we'll see how arrogant you are, my

girl. You won't be strutting about then with your shirt hanging out –

DENIS: SHE GETS THE PICTURE!

PHILIPPE: (*Startled.*) What?

DENIS: (*To BETTY.*) You get the general gist of what he's saying, am I right?

PHILIPPE: What the fuck's this to do with him? Who asked his opinion?

DENIS: You've been getting on my nerves all night! I'm a patient man but I've got my limits – and you've just reached them!

PHILIPPE: Bugger off!!

DENIS: One more word and I'll ram this chair down your throat!

PHILIPPE: (*To HENRI.*) Sack this man immediately!

DENIS: AAAH!

DENIS picks up a chair and rushes at PHILIPPE, almost knocking him to the floor.

MADAME MENARD: AAAHHH!

PHILIPPE: HELP!!

BETTY: DENIS, STOP IT!

YOLANDE: NO, NO!

BETTY struggles to hold DENIS back as YOLANDE rushes to PHILIPPE who's in a state of shock. MADAME MENARD is swaying slightly on her feet. PHILIPPE stands behind YOLANDE.

PHILIPPE: Who – who – who the fuck does he think he is??

DENIS: I warned you! When I get angry, I'm psychotic!

PHILIPPE: (*To HENRI.*) Aren't you going to do something??
(*Pause.*) Henri??

All eyes turn to HENRI who hasn't moved throughout.

HENRI: No. I'm not going to do something. Fuck your
problems. I've had enough. I'm tired. I just want to lock
up and go to bed.

PHILIPPE stares at HENRI.

PHILIPPE: 'Fuck my problems'. Thanks a lot.

HENRI: That's right. Fuck 'em. D'you care about mine?
Do you even know anything about my problems?? Apart
from your stupid TV show – which I didn't even see by
the way – have you any…consideration at all?

PHILIPPE: 'Consideration…'? What's that supposed to
mean??

HENRI: Aha! See? He doesn't know what it means either!

*HENRI shakes his head in small triumph. DENIS lets go of
the chair.*

DENIS: (*To HENRI.*) If you don't need me any more,
boss… I'd like to get off.

HENRI: No, no, sure, off you go. Thanks…for helping out.

DENIS: 'S nothing. (*To BETTY.*) Fancy a quiet drink
somewhere? Just you and me.

BETTY: Why not?

She moves towards the entrance and stops.

(*To the family.*) See you around.

No reply from PHILIPPE or from MADAME MENARD.

YOLANDE: 'Bye, Betty.

BETTY: Take care. (*To HENRI.*) 'Bye.

They kiss goodbye.

HENRI: See you.

BETTY starts to go. DENIS is alongside but stops.

DENIS: This boyfriend…he's not the bloke who works at your brother's bar by any chance, is he?

She steps up to him. They kiss. The others look on in varying degrees of amazement.

YOLANDE: Oh my my my!

BETTY and DENIS leave the bar arm in arm.

HENRI: Shit. Betty and Denis. I had my suspicions… always rabbiting on to each other… Shit.

MADAME MENARD: *He's* the 'someone special'??

HENRI: Well…why not, eh?

YOLANDE: I knew they were friends. But not such good ones! I had no idea. (*To PHILIPPE.*) Did you? (*No reply.*) He's part of the family now. He's my brother-in-law! (*To MADAME MENARD.*) He's your son-in-law! He's –

MADAME MENARD: Yes, yes, thank you, Yoyo.

The sound of DENIS's motorbike going past. HENRI watches them go.

MADAME MENARD: Everyone's emotionally exhausted. Time we went home.

YOLANDE: She's a lucky girl, Betty. I think Denis is very nice.

HENRI: Uh uh.

PHILIPPE: Let's go, come on.

PHILIPPE drops YOLANDE's bag and coat on the table in front of her. He holds up MADAME MENARD's coat for her to put on.

Ready when you are, Mum.

MADAME MENARD: (*To HENRI.*) 'Bye bye, sweetheart. And don't worry. Everything will work out.

HENRI: 'Course it will.

MADAME MENARD puts her coat on.

MADAME MENARD: She wouldn't even talk to you?

HENRI: No.

MADAME MENARD: Mummy told you not to go.

HENRI: Yeah, you did.

MADAME MENARD: So…next Friday then?

HENRI: Next Friday.

MADAME MENARD: Doesn't Mummy get a kiss?

He kisses her.

Try not to worry.

She smiles at him and goes towards the door. PHILIPPE and HENRI mutter their goodbyes with routine kisses. PHILIPPE is about to leave with MADAME MENARD when he remembers that he came with YOLANDE. He turns back to her.

PHILIPPE: You coming or what?

YOLANDE is getting her coat on in her own good time. She smiles at HENRI.

YOLANDE: Can't we help you clear up, Henri?

HENRI: No, no, I'll do it in the morning. I get up early, y'know?

PHILIPPE: Yoyo.

YOLANDE: I'm coming.

PHILIPPE: Well, come on then.

YOLANDE: I said I'm coming! Give me a second, for heaven's sake!

PHILIPPE and MADAME MENARD leave. YOLANDE is about to follow but then steps back nearer to HENRI.

Nobody said anything about the duck...but it was delicious. And I know my duck.

HENRI: That's...sweet of you.

YOLANDE: No it's true. It was delicious.

They kiss goodbye. YOLANDE leaves with a little wave. HENRI is now on his own. He turns the lights out. He goes over to the jukebox. He's about to switch it off but decides to select a record instead. After a moment, we hear a scratchy old recording of Caruso singing 'Una Furtiva Lagrima'. HENRI goes over to the dog.

HENRI: I don't think today's the day we start singing again, is it?

HENRI turns out the last of the lights. Just the light from the jukebox and from the street outside. Suddenly the phone rings. HENRI wanders over and answers it.

(*Into phone.*) Yeah? Oh. Arlette. Uh, yeah, yeah. They just left. Yeah, you know. (*Pause.*) Oh. You liked that, did you? You didn't...think I looked like a prick then? Your neighbours, y'know...? I don't know...things can change I think... I mean, *I* can change. What? Sure, I know I am but... (*Shouts.*) I SAID I CAN CHANGE, DIDN'T I?? Sorry, sorry...yeah...uh, Arlette, listen...uh...you know what I think we should do? (*Pause.*) An English-type pub...yep, I think so too...somewhere people'd want to come back to...

The music gets louder. Fade.

The End.